Attainment's
Safety Skills
Reader

Tom Kinney

Illustrated by Gabe Eltaeb

The CD-ROM contains a printable
version of the entire book in the PDF file
SafetySkills.pdf
Adobe Acrobat Reader is required to
view or print this file and can be
installed from the CD-ROM.

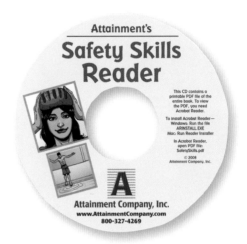

Author: Tom Kinney
Illustrator: Gabe Eltaeb
Concept: Beverly Potts
Graphic Design: Sherry Pribbenow

An Attainment Publication

ISBN 1-57861-656-5

Attainment Company, Inc.

P.O. Box 930160
Verona, Wisconsin 53593-0160
Phone 800-327-4269   Fax 800.942.3865

www.AttainmentCompany.com

Table of Contents   Community

Table of Contents   Home

Table of Contents   Home

Table of Contents   Home

Table of Contents   Recreational

Table of Contents   Personal

Introduction

Safety Skills Reader looks at essential everyday safety skills in the context of the locations in which their application is required. To this end, it presents four color-coded chapters with stories blessed with original art by well-known illustrator, Gabe Eltaeb. Chapters include: Community, Home, Recreation, and Personal. The book can be given directly to users to read, or you can print out the assigned pages from the PDF of the book which is provided on CD-ROM. Your third option is to photocopy assigned pages from the spiralbound book.

There are 26 topics, each looking at key areas of safety skills and followed by an activity page with vocabulary from the stories and multiple choice comprehension questions. This presentation is standardized throughout the book.

Who is Safety Skills Reader Intended For?

Its primary audience are adolescents and adults who read at a second grade level or below. Younger readers down to ages 14-16 in transition classes will also find stories age appropriate. Subject matter corresponds to that being taught in transition classes everywhere. There are three ways students can use this book:

1. **Student reads independently.** Students independently read the stories and answer student questions.

2. **Student reads with assistance.** Students read the stories with the encouragement and oversight of a tutor or instructor. When completing study questions, instructors can give hints to struggling students.

3. **Tutor reads story to student.** The student listens to the story being read by the instructor. The instructor encourages participation by repeatedly pointing to and discussing the content of illustrations. Study questions are read to the student who can answer verbally or with accommodations.

Additional Instructional Activities

In addition to the merging of safety skill instruction with reading comprehension, there are several instructional activities you can incorporate:

1. Find examples of functional sight words in the text and compile corresponding vocabulary lists for each student. If you have time, you can also make individual sight word cards for independent study for each student.

2. Link community outings to relevant topics like "Pedestrian Safety" and discuss with students.

3. Give homework assignments by simply reproducing stories and lessons and sending them along with students at the end of the school day.

Aligning to Standards and IEP Objectives

Recent national trends toward setting universal achievement standards have helped energize literacy instruction for students with cognitive disabilities. In the process, there has been an increased emphasis on aligning instruction to standards through IEPs. Examples of appropriate standards could include:

1. Identifying themes from the text

2. Responding to comprehension questions

3. Retelling stories in sequence

4. Writing about reading materials

Writing to Student IEPs

The areas of literacy and life skill instruction are often addressed in student IEPs. Safety Skills Reader makes a point of covering numerous daily living activities as well as community and vocational skill areas for transition students. Instructors will find that using the study questions to write measurable goals and objectives to student IEPs works well. Sample IEP objectives and benchmarks are included below:

Safety Skills Objectives

1. Student will read and answer questions to each story.

   a. Will predict content based upon title, illustration, or caption

   b. Will read the story

   c. Will locate information and answer the questions

2. With prompts will read the story and answer questions.

   a. With prompts will predict content based upon title, illustration, or caption

   b. With prompts will locate information and answer the questions

3. Will listen to the story and answer the questions read.

   a. With prompts will predict content based upon title, illustration, or caption

   b. Will listen to the story

   c. Will listen to and answer questions read

Community

Walking is a fun way to see sights and a good way to get exercise. But it is important to walk the streets safely because accidents can happen there.

People who walk the streets by foot are called pedestrians.

When you cross the street, first look left, right, then left again. Keep looking until you reach the other side.

Cross streets only at corners. Use crosswalks and traffic lights if you can.

When you cross the street make eye contact with drivers, so you can see what they are doing. And to make sure they see you.

Wear something that glows in the dark when walking at night. Buy clip-on reflective red lights to wear after dark.

When there is no sidewalk, walk facing traffic on the edge of the road. Stay as far to the left of the road as you can.

Name _____ Date _____

Pedestrian Safety

pedestrian — a person who travels by foot
crosswalk — a place where pedestrians cross the street
reflective — a surface that reflects light

Directions: Circle the answer

1. When walking on city streets, be careful because:
    a. accidents can happen there
    b. you might get lost
    c. you might get hungry

2. When crossing the street:
    a. look right, left, then right again
    b. look for movie stars crossing with you
    c. look left, right, then left again

3. Cross streets:
    a. any time you please
    b. only at corners
    c. in the middle of the block

We spend a lot of time in cars. It is fun and necessary to take car rides, but there are many dangers to be aware of.

Make sure the car isn't moving when you get in.

Be careful getting in the car when it is hot outside. Use your hand to feel the seat so you don't burn yourself. Wearing a shirt and long pants helps.

Look at the height of the door and bend down getting in so you don't bump your head.

Make sure your fingers are clear of the door when you shut it.
And be careful you don't get your clothes caught.

Make sure your seat allows you leg room. Sitting for long periods
in a cramped position can cause discomfort.

Buckle your safety belt as soon as you sit. Different cars have different seat belts. Know how each works before the driver takes off.

Don't use the radio or CD player unless you ask the driver first. It may distract the person driving.

Before you roll the window down, ask the driver. He may have the heat or air conditioner on, or have other reasons.

Don't put hands or feet out of the window when the car is moving. Don't get out until it has stopped and the engine is off.

Community

Name _____ Date _____

Passenger Safety

discomfort — feeling ill at ease
distract — to take your attention away from something else
engine — motor that converts energy into work

Directions: Circle the answer.

1. When you get in a car in hot weather:
    a. jump right in
    b. feel the seat with your hand to see if it is hot
    c. enjoy the air conditioner

2. Buckle your seat belt:
    a. after the car starts moving
    b. wait 10 minutes first
    c. as soon as you sit down

3. Use the radio or CD player:
    a. any time you want
    b. ask the driver first
    c. to play your own CDs

It's fun and good exercise to ride bicycles. But it is easy to have accidents with them.

Always wear a bike helmet. Make sure it is tightly fastened. Head injuries are a common bicycle injury.

Make sure you keep your bicycle in good condition. Keep up on its maintenance.

Always keep both hands on the handlebars. The only exception is when you are going to signal for a turn.

Try to avoid the most busy streets.

When you come to an intersection of a busy street, walk your bike across it.

Let people and cars go first.

Don't ride double or hitch rides on other vehicles.

Don't ride between two vehicles and don't swerve in and out of traffic.

Wear bright clothes and reflectors when it is dark outside.

Name _____ Date _____

Bicycle Safety

maintenance — keeping something in good working condition
exception — something that doesn't follow the usual rules
reflectors — a red piece of glass worn by the bicyclist that motorists can see at night

Directions: Circle the answer.

1. When biking, always wear:
   a. a helmet
   b. clothes
   c. a swim suit

2. Make sure your bicycle is:
   a. cool looking
   b. red
   c. in top condition

3. It is _____ to ride double:
   1. dangerous
   2. fun
   3. exciting

When you go places by yourself you enjoy your freedom and have a good time. But there is also a chance you might get lost.

There are things you can do to keep yourself safe if you are not sure where you are.

Always make sure you have identification with you.

If you use a "talker" always make sure you have one with you.

If you have a cell phone make sure you have it with you.

Don't be afraid. If you panic it will only make things worse.

Getting Lost   4

Don't wander around. Stay in areas where there are other people.

Look for people who can help you, like a police officer.
Look for people doing something. Find a clerk in a store or
someone at a desk.

Show someone you trust your identification and tell them you are lost.

Name _____ Date _____

Getting Lost

freedom — the ability to do what you want
identification — proof of who you are
panic — a strong and often sudden feeling of fear

Directions: Circle the answer.

1. When out in the community alone, make sure you have:
    a. plenty of money
    b. a gun
    c. identification

2. Stay in areas where there are:
    a. other people
    b. lots of wild animals
    c. dangerous looking people

3. If you are lost, look for:
    a. others who are also lost
    b. dangerous looking people
    c. those who can help, like a police officer

Having a job helps you earn money and gives you the freedom to live on your own. But be aware of safety issues on the job.

Young people don't always get their choice of jobs. You might get a job where there are risks.

Many young workers don't get safety training on the job. Ask your employers for safety training if available.

Young workers often don't know their rights and are afraid to ask questions. Know your rights and ask questions.

Community

Specific Job Safety
These risks happen in the following jobs:

Food Service: Dangers include sharp objects and heated surfaces. Slippery floors can be risky. Move slowly and carefully when in these conditions.

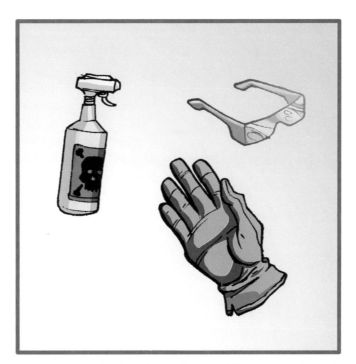

Janitorial: Dangers include cleaning with toxic chemicals. Ask your employer for protective gloves and eye gear.

Retail: Dangers include lifting heavy objects. Test the weight before lifting it. This will tell you if you can lift without risk.

Clerical: Dangers include repetitive strain injuries when you repeat the same motions. Guards help you avoid these.

Name _____ Date _____

Work Safety

issue — a point or matter of discussion
employer — someone who hires and manages workers
protective — intended to keep you safe from some danger

Directions: Circle the answer.

1. Getting a job helps you:
   a. feel responsible
   b. make money
   c. have a sense of freedom
   d. all of the above

2. Dangers in retail jobs include:
   a. getting bored
   b. making too much money
   c. becoming a victim of violent crimes

3. Dangers in computer data entry include:
   a. falling asleep on the job
   b. repetitive strain injuries
   c. back injuries

Home

There are many reasons why you may need to start a fire.
But if you do, take these safety precautions.

Make sure your home has as many smoke alarms as it needs.
Test them often and replace batteries twice a year.

Home

Matches and candles should be kept in safe places out of reach of small children.

Keep a fire extinguisher where it is easy to find and near to fire sources. Make sure it rates for grease and electric fires.

Home

If you allow people to smoke, make sure cigarettes are put out before you dump the ashes.

Make sure your electrical wiring has been checked recently by an electrician.

Use space heaters with caution. Keep flammable objects away from them. Never leave them on when you are sleeping.

If you use a fireplace, have the chimney and fireplace checked and cleaned on a regular basis.

Unplug appliances when you are not using them.

Plan an escape from each part of your house. Make a map of this plan and practice it once a year.

Name _____ Date _____

Fire Safety

precaution — an action taken to prevent a problem
electrician — skilled tradesman who works with electrical equipment
flammable — objects that easily catch on fire

Directions: Circle the answer.

1. Test your smoke alarms often and:
   a. replace their batteries twice a year
   b. put in new batteries once a year
   c. don't worry about new batteries

2. Make sure your fire extinguisher:
   a. is really expensive
   b. is really cheap
   c. rates for grease and electric fires

3. Have your electrical wiring tested by:
   a. a plumber
   b. a door to door salesman
   c. an electrician

Home

You need access to a clean and safe bathroom. But accidents can happen there and disease can be spread.

Make sure water spilled on the floor is wiped up to avoid wet spots that cause falls.

Put lids back on medications and return the container to a place out of the reach of children.

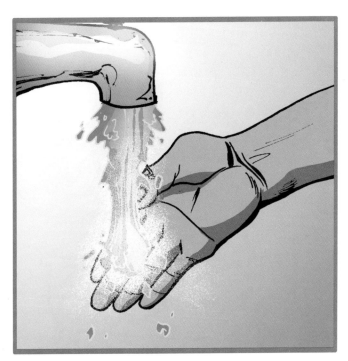

Check temperature when pouring water to make sure it isn't too hot.

Be careful when getting in bath or shower so you don't slip.
Put skid resistant products on the tub and shower floors.

Water and electricity don't mix. Don't use outlets when using
water. Unplug hair dryers and appliances when not in use.

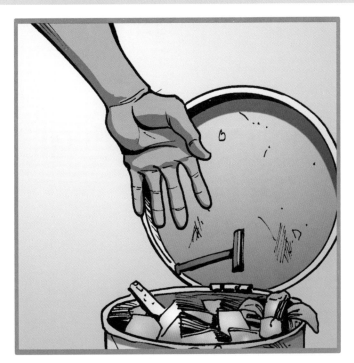

Don't throw safety razors in the bathroom garbage. Put them where children can not reach them.

Dirty toilets spread disease. Use proper cleaning materials on them and keep those materials in locked containers.

Home

Name _____ Date _____

Bathroom Safety

medications — all kinds of medicines
temperature — the degree of heat or cold
resistant — able to tolerate certain conditions

Directions: Circle the answer.

1. Wipe up spilled water because:
    a. it can cause falls
    b. you can't drink it anyway
    c. it might run into the next room

2. Don't use hair dryers while:
    a. watching TV
    b. driving a car
    c. using water

3. Dirty toilets spread:
    a. gossip
    b. disease
    c. bad feelings

Home

Medicine cabinets often store drugs and other dangerous items like razor blades.

Keep medications in original containers. When medicines are put in the wrong bottles they can make you sick.

Home

Clean out the medicine cabinet at least once or twice a year.

Don't keep medications in the bathroom unless it is well ventilated. Moist environments cause them to break down.

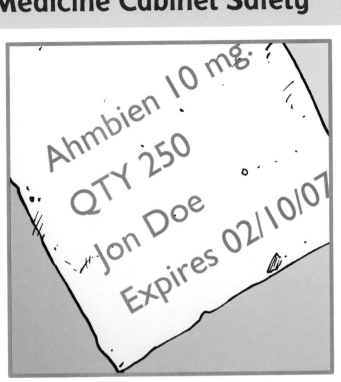

Check labels on medicines and throw out old ones. Ask your doctor how long to keep certain medications.

When you throw out medications, don't flush them down the toilet. They can get into your drinking water and harm you.

Home

Read the label carefully to be sure you have the right bottle.

Don't use the medicine cabinet to store cleaning items.
Contact lens cleaners are okay.

If you keep razors in your medicine cabinet, make sure the sharp edges don't stick out.

Name _____ Date _____

Medicine Cabinet Safety

cabinet — a storage compartment
ventilate — to keep air moving so it's fresh
label — put on medicine bottles to tell you what is in it

Directions: Circle the answer.

1. Keep medications in:
    a. original containers
    b. the wastebasket
    c. the freezer

2. Don't throw medications:
    a. at your friends
    b. at your neighbors
    c. down the toilet

3. Don't put cleaning items:
    a. in medicine bottles
    b. in the medicine cabinet
    c. in the refrigerator

Home

Safety Skills Reader

Stoves and ovens help prepare foods. But they can cause serious burns if you are not careful.

Stove tops have gas flames or electric elements. Make sure nothing flammable is near the burner.

Home

Keep pot and pan handles away from places where they can be bumped or small children can reach them.

Use oven mitts or pot holders when removing pan lids or holding pan handles. Carry pans slowly and carefully.

Home

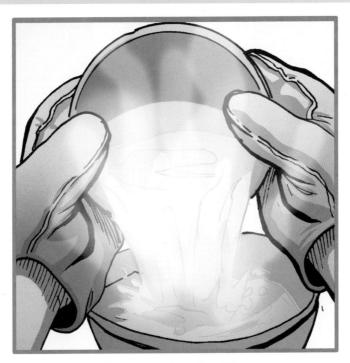

Pour boiling water out of a pan slowly. The steam can get in your eyes if you're not careful.

Use oven mitts when taking food out of the oven.

Home

Be very careful when taking food out of the microwave. Foods can release a lot of heat when their cover is removed.

Wait for the food to cool before removing the lid. Or carefully remove the lid with a pot holder or oven mitt.

Name _____ Date _____

Kitchen/Dining Room Safety

serious — dangerous, causing fear and anxiety
elements — wires in electric appliances, like stoves

Directions: Circle the answer.

1. Don't put flammable items:
   a. on the table
   b. in the refrigerator
   c. near stove burners

2. Pour boiling water slowly because:
   a. it's more fun that way
   b. its steam can get in your eyes
   c. it pours better that way

3. Wait for food to cool before removing pot lids because:
   a. foods release a lot of heat
   b. it tastes better that way
   c. pot lids slide off better when they are cool

Home

Meals are times to enjoy sharing food and the company of family and friends. But problems can arise during meals.

Talk about things everyone is interested in and try to avoid arguments. Meals can be times when people get into fights.

Home

Chew slowly and thoroughly before swallowing.

Be careful when eating hot food. Give it time to cool off before you start to eat.

Keep liquids and hot foods away from the edge of tables when you are setting and serving food.

When passing hot dishes around the table be careful.
Use a pot holder if necessary.

Home

When using a knife to cut foods like meat be aware of its sharp edge and point it away from your hand.

Name _____ Date _____

Mealtime — Eating Safety

argument — a discussion with both sides disagreeing
thorough — careful and complete

Directions: Circle the answer.

1. When sharing a meal, try to avoid:
   a. arguments
   b. talking
   c. fist fights

2. Chew:
   a. quickly
   b. with your mouth open
   c. slowly and thoroughly

3. When cutting food, point the knife:
   a. away from your hand
   b. toward your hand
   c. at your meal guests

Home

The kitchen is one of the most used rooms in the house and is where the most accidents happen.

There is still a lot of work to do after the meal is finished. Remove all dishes and leftover food from the table.

Home

Cover and chill leftover food quickly in shallow dishes. Food left out of the refrigerator too long can cause food poisoning.

Pick up sharp utensils like knives securely by the handles when clearing the table.

Avoid using throw rugs in the kitchen. You could slip and drop hot food or sharp utensils.

Name _____ Date _____

Putting Food Away

leftovers — food you didn't eat but want to save
shallow — measuring little from top to bottom
utensils — tools you use to eat or serve with, like forks and spoons

Directions: Circle the answer.
1. Most home accidents happen in:
    a. the bathroom
    b. bedrooms
    c. the kitchen

2. Food left too long out of the refrigerator:
    a. can cause food poisoning
    b. tastes better
    c. isn't a problem

3. Pick up sharp knives by:
    a. the blade
    b. any way you can
    c. the handle

Home

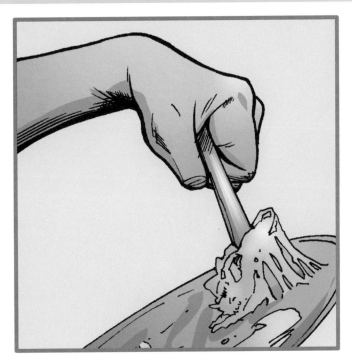

Be sure to scrape excess food from the dishes before putting them in water.

Soak pots and pans in soapy warm water as soon as you are done cooking. This will make them easier to wash.

Scrub dishes in soapy warm water. Test water temperature first.

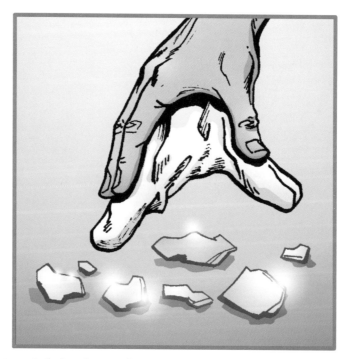

Do not try to pick broken glass pieces out of the sink.
Drain the water first and use a paper towel to pick them up.

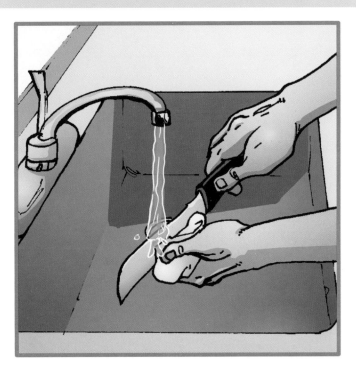

Don't throw sharp knives into a full sink. You might grab one by mistake and cut yourself. Wash them separately.

Name _____ Date _____

Doing Dishes by Hand

scrape — to rub a surface clean
excess — too much of something
separate — to keep apart

Directions: Circle the answer.

1. Scrape excess food from dishes before:
   a. putting them in water to wash
   b. licking the plate clean
   c. throwing them away

2. If you break glass in the sink:
   a. pick it up by hand
   b. use a fork to pick it up
   c. use a towel to pick it up

3. When washing sharp knives by hand:
   a. wash them separately
   b. throw them in with everything else
   c. just reach in the soapy water and grab them

Home

Dishwashers save time and improve kitchen hygiene. But they also pose dangers you can easily avoid.

Be careful not to overload your dishwasher. That can cause it to jam and not work.

Make sure small items and plastic items are secure so they don't fall on the dishwasher heating element.

Do not leave home when the dishwasher is running. If it overflows you can't do anything about it.

Make sure it is done working before you go to bed.

Name _____ Date _____

Dishwasher Safety

hygiene — the practice of cleanliness
overload — too big a load
overflow — to flow or run over the top

Directions: Circle the answer.

1. If you overload your dishwasher:
    a. it could jam and not work
    b. don't worry about it
    c. you can get more dishes in

2. Make sure small or plastic items:
    a. are kept out of your dishwasher
    b. are cheap before you buy them
    c. are secure

3. Make sure your dishwasher:
    a. is done running before you leave home or go to bed
    b. has pretty colors before you buy it
    c. is expensive

Home

Clothes washers and dryers save regular trips to the laundromat. But they do pose safety issues.

Washers

Be careful when putting clothes in. Make sure you balance and level the load so your washer does not tilt and stop working.

Home

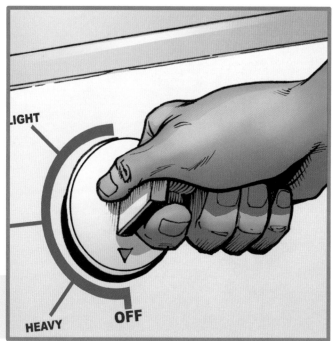

Washers

Make sure the washer is off before you leave the house or go to bed.

Washers

Keep the area around your washer free of combustible items.

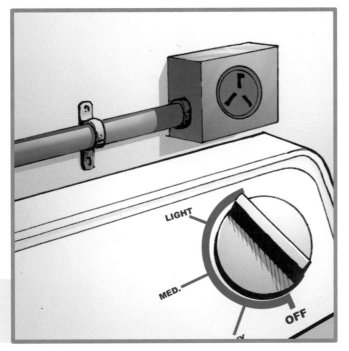

Washers

Be sure you have an outlet that can handle your washer.
Washers use a lot of electricity. Electrical overload can cause fires.

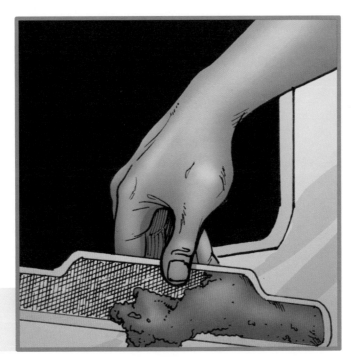

Dryers

Remove lint filter buildup every time you use your dryer.

Home

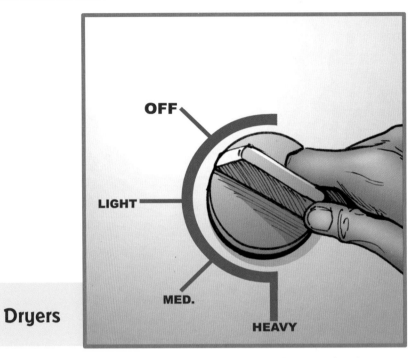

Dryers

Make sure the dryer is off before you leave the house or go to bed.

Dryers

Keep the area around your dryer free of combustible items.

Home

Dryers

Be sure you have an outlet that can handle your dryer. Dryers use a lot of electricity and overload can cause fires.

Home

Name _____ Date _____

Clothes Washer/Dryer Safety

laundromat — a place where you pay to wash your own clothes
balance — making sure the washer or dryer has an equal load on all sides
combustible— easily able to catch fire

Directions: Circle the answer.

1. Balance the load so:
    a. it looks nice
    b. it doesn't tilt and stop working
    c. white clothes are on the same side

2. Make sure the washer or dryer is off:
    a. before you put clothes in
    b. after you put clothes in
    c. before you leave the house or go to bed

3. Make sure your outlet:
    a. can handle your washer
    b. is indoors
    c. isn't underwater

Home

Garbage disposals are handy tools. But they do require safety precautions.

Batch disposals are activated by turning a stopper. Feed disposals activate by flipping a wall switch. Know which you have.

Home

A common problem with garbage disposals is food materials packed so tight the blades can't rotate.

Never put your hand in the disposal.

Home

Before you do anything else, turn off the power at your main power grid.

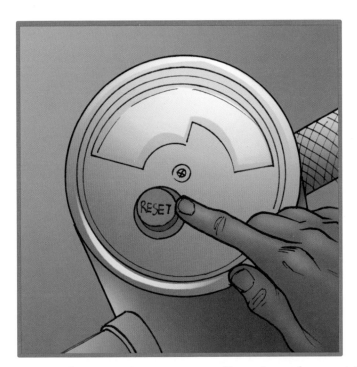

Wait five minutes after turning power off and push reset button.

Use tongs or pliers to remove food or whatever is clogging it.

If that doesn't help, call a repair person.

Name _____ Date _____

Garbage Disposal Safety

activate — to set in motion
rotate — to move in a circle

Directions: Circle the answer.

1. Problems with disposals include:
    a. leaves, tree branches, and stumps
    b. food materials packed too tightly
    c. dirt, sand, and oily water

2. When the garbage disposal stops working:
    a. turn the power off at your main power grid
    b. open a soda and take a break
    c. run out of the house

3. It nothing works:
    a. give up
    b. scream at the top of your lungs
    c. call a repair person

Home

It is fun to be at home by yourself. But when people you do not know call or come to the door be prepared.

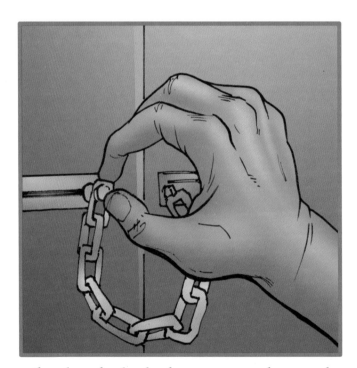

Always keep the door locked when you are home alone.

Keep outside and inside lights on at night.

Make sure all windows are locked shut.

Home

If someone calls and says something bad or obscene hang the phone up. Then call the police.

Some people will try to sell you things over the phone. Just say "I am not interested" and hang up.

If someone you do not know comes to the door do not let them in.

Leave the door chain attached so you can open the door and see who it is. If you do not know them do not let them in.

Name _____ Date _____

Strangers at Home

obscene — bad or offensive language

Directions: Circle the answer.

1. When you are home alone and someone comes to the door:
   a. be prepared
   b. let them in
   c. call the police immediately

2. Always keep the door:
   a. open
   b. shut but unlocked
   c. locked

3. If someone says something bad on the phone:
   a. hang up, then call the police
   b. say something rude to them
   c. keep listening

Hand and power tools help you do hard jobs and save you time. But they can be dangerous too.

Keep tools safety stored in a garage or shed to protect them from the elements. Tools in good shape work better and are safer.

Home

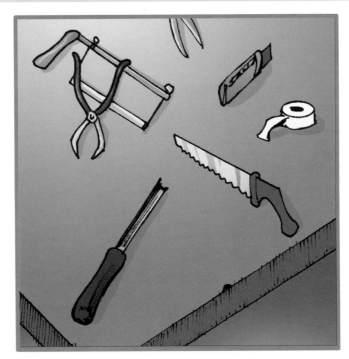

Don't leave tools laying around. Clean tools and put them on a tool rack.

Keep tool handles in good shape. A tool head that breaks off can cause injury. Inspect every time you use them.

Home

Cutting edges should be kept sharp with hand and power tools. Dull edges cause accidents.

Most power tools have safety guards. Check regularly to see if your guards are in working shape.

Home

Wear protective eyewear when using power tools or cutting tools.

Name _____ Date _____

Hand/Power Tool Safety

elements — natural things like rain that can ruin your tools
inspect — look at, see what condition something is in

Directions: Circle the answer.

1. Keep tools:
    a. outside the house
    b. in a garage or shed
    c. in your bedroom

2. Tools should be:
    a. safely on tool racks
    b. in your bed
    c. on the kitchen table

3. When using power or cutting tools:
    a. don't worry about a thing, just go for it
    b. wear protective eyewear
    c. wear loose fitting shirts

Home

To live independently you will need electrical appliances.
They are very helpful. But they can be dangerous.

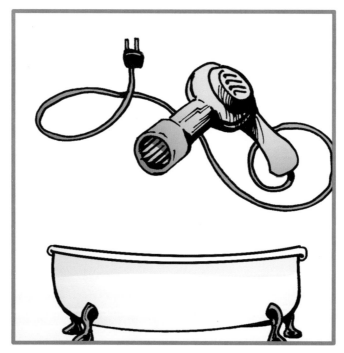

Keep electrical appliances like hair dryers away from sinks, tubs,
or other areas filled with water.

Before you clean an electric appliance first make sure you unplug it.

Be careful not to overload your outlets with too many electric cords.

If your appliances often short out or fuses blow call a repairman.
You might need to have wiring or circuits replaced.

Never run electrical cords under carpets or rugs. They can overheat
and start a fire.

Home

Don't force appliance plugs into outlets if they don't fit easily.

If your plug is three-way, make sure all three are plugged in.
Don't force it into the outlet.

If you notice a wire is frayed don't use it. Instead, have it replaced.
It could cause a short.

Be aware of electrical lines that come into your house.
Know where they are, buried or overhead.

Home

Name _____ Date _____

Electrical Safety

appliance — household devices operated by gas or electricity
outlet — wall plug-ins for electric devices
circuit — a device that provides a path for electrical current to flow

Directions: Circle the answer.

1. Keep electrical appliances away from:
   a. sinks, tubs, or other household things that hold water
   b. garages, tool sheds, and basements
   c. electrical outlets

2. If your appliances keep shorting out:
   a. stop using them
   b. call your mother
   c. call the repairman

3. If you run electrical cords under a carpet:
   a. they can overheat and start a fire
   b. it helps to hide them
   c. you might have trouble finding them

Home

Recreational

Nothing is more fun than relaxing in a lake or a pool. But keep safety in mind.

If you don't know how to swim, take lessons. Everyone should know how to swim.

Drowning happens when your lungs fill with water. It can take less than two minutes. Be aware when you are near water.

Never dive off the side of the pool. Don't dive in the water when you are outdoors, unless swimmers are allowed to.

Test the water before going in. If it's cold, it can make muscles stiff. Or cause you to open your mouth and swallow water.

Never go swimming by yourself.

When swimming, know what's on the bottom. Walk in slowly. Look for grass and weeds because they can trap you.

When in the ocean, be sure there is a lifeguard. Be careful with strong waves because they can knock you down.

Recreational

Don't go swimming in the dark or during a storm.
If you get a cramp, get out of the water right away.

Even if you are a good swimmer, always be careful. Many things besides sharks can put you in danger.

Name _____ Date _____

Swimming Safety

drowning — when lungs fill with water causing suffocation and death
shock — a sudden disturbance
cramp — painful muscle contraction

Directions: Circle the answer.

1. If you don't know how to swim:
   a. don't worry about it
   b. jump in the water anyway
   c. take lessons

2. Never go swimming:
   a. by yourself
   b. in large bodies of water
   c. in your kitchen sink

3. Large ocean waves can:
   a. give you something to surf on
   b. be exciting
   c. knock you down

We enjoy being in the sun. It is our main source of vitamin D. But too much sun can cause skin cancer.

Sun damage hurts some people more than others. The lighter the skin color, the more it can cause damage.

Sun rays are the strongest from 10 a.m. to 4 p.m. Limit your time in the sun during these hours.

Protect yourself from sun rays by covering up. This is the easiest ways to protect yourself from the sun.

Use sunscreen. It comes in many forms, like gels, lotions, and sprays. Make sure the sunscreen has at least an SPF 15 rating.

Too much exposure to sun causes eye damage.
Protective eyewear helps reduce damage from sun exposure.

Some medications make skin more sensitive to UV rays. Ask your doctor If you are on any of these medicines.

If you do get a sunburn, put aloe vera gel on it. For the worst areas, use a 1% hydrocortisone cream.

Recreational

Name _____ Date _____

Sun Safety

vitamin — key nutrients the body needs
exposure — vulnerability to the elements
sensitive — overly responsive to stimuli

Directions: Circle the answer.

1. Sun is our main source of:
    a. heat
    b. sunburn
    c. vitamin D

2. Sun rays are the strongest between:
    a. 10 a.m. to 4 p.m.
    b. midnight and dawn
    c. 4 p.m. and 5 p.m.

3. If you get a sunburn:
    a. don't worry, stay out in the sun
    b. put on aloe vera or hydrocortisone cream
    c. don't ever go back in the sun

In climates where it gets cold it is necessary to be prepared. There are things you can do to be ready.

Make sure you have proper winter wear before the first cold day. You never know when that will be.

Winter wear includes warm coats and clothing, headwear, footwear and gloves.

Pay attention to weather channels on the radio and television. That way you will know when bad weather is on the way.

Stay home if it is too cold or blizzard conditions are expected.

If you feel you must go outside dress warmly and cover your mouth to protect your lungs.

Be careful not to work too fast if you are shovelling snow. Cold conditions can cause stress.

Walk slowly and carefully on icy surfaces. Make sure your footwear gives you traction.

Name _____ Date _____

Cold Weather Safety

climate — average weather in an area
blizzard — heavy winter storm
traction — to grip the surface without slipping

Directions: Circle the answer.

1. Winter wear includes:
   a. sandals, swim suits, and a beach towel
   b. warm coats, headwear, footwear, and gloves
   c. a light jacket and a baseball cap

2. If blizzard conditions are expected:
   a. stay home
   b. go out
   c. put on a light coat and go for it

3. When walking on ice surfaces:
   a. walk slowly and carefully and wear shoes with traction
   b. skate on the ice, it's faster
   c. walk quickly, you get there faster

Sports are fun and great exercise. Just make sure you observe basic safety rules.

Wear the right helmet for the sport. It should have a Consumer Product Safety Commission sticker. Be sure it fits.

Make sure you have protective eye equipment.

If you play contact sports like basketball, get a mouthguard. If you wear a retainer, remove it and replace it with your mouthguard.

Wrist, knee, and elbow guards help, especially if you have an injury in one of those areas.

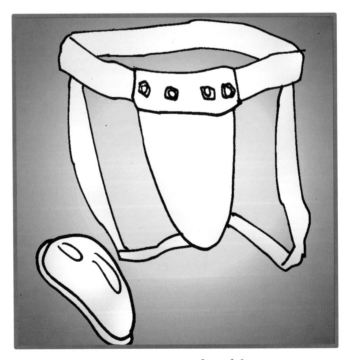

When playing contact sports, men should wear a protective cup.

Wear the right footwear for the sport and make sure it fits.
For example, special shoes are made for runners.

Never exercise until you do warm ups and stretch. Do light jogging,
walking, or jumping jacks. Learn stretching from trainers.

Recreational

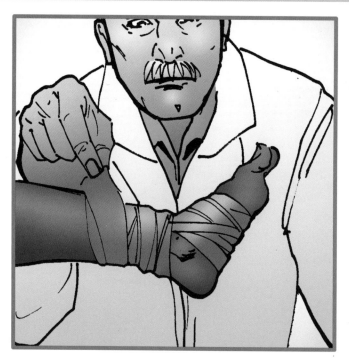

Do not play or if you have an injury. Wait until it is healed or your doctor tells you it is okay.

Learn the rules of the game. Rules are made to keep the game safe.

Name _____ Date _____

Sports Safety

equipment — a tool or device that helps you do something

retainer — dental appliance that holds teeth in place

stretching — exercises to keep muscles loose and prevent injury

Directions: Circle the answer.

1. Wear the right helmet:
   a. for the latest fashion craze
   b. with your team's colors
   c. for the sport you are playing

2. If you play contact sports:
   a. get ready to be hurt
   b. wear a mouthguard
   c. hit them before they hit you

3. Don't exercise until:
   a. you have stretched first
   b. the game is over
   c. you are full of energy

We enjoy being outdoors in nice weather. But that is also when bugs are out.

Be careful in places where insects go. They like stagnant water, blooming flowers, and uncovered food.

Stay away from scented products like lotions, perfumes, and hair sprays. They attract bugs.

When you see a stinging insect like a bee or hornet, remain calm and move away from it slowly.

Recreational

Bees leave a stinger in you. Remove by softly scraping it with a fingernail. If you can't take it out, don't worry.

Insecticides with DEET in it work well and are safe. Many common brands have it.

Don't use too much insecticide and don't put it on your face.
Put more on every one to two hours.

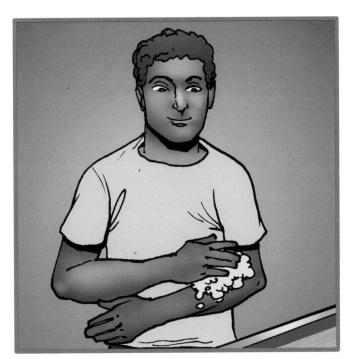

When you come inside to stay, wash insecticide off with soap
and water.

Name _____ Date _____

Bug Safety

stagnant — stale water that doesn't move
insecticide — product to kill or keep bugs away

Directions: Circle the answer.

1. Insects go places like:
    a. shopping malls
    b. city streets
    c. stagnant water, flowers, and uncovered food

2. When you see a stinging insect:
    a. grab it to see if it really stings
    b. remain calm and move away slowly
    c. run away as fast as you can

3. Don't put insecticide:
    a. on your face
    b. on your arms
    c. on your legs

Personal

You enjoy meeting your friends in public places and at parties. But there are risks you must watch out for.

Public Places

Shopping malls are busy areas with many people you don't know. Because you don't know them, you must be careful.

Stay in open places where friends and other people are. Don't ever leave with someone you don't know.

Don't be rude to strangers who come up to you. Just tell them firmly that you don't talk to people you don't know.

Personal

Stay away from fights and gang members. Stay with your friends and move quickly away from trouble.

Some people use drugs and might offer them to you. Don't let others influence you.

At Parties

If you have trusted friends who can go with you to a party, invite them along. It will help you avoid temptation.

If someone you don't trust offers you something to drink or eat, just tell them 'no thanks.'

Personal

Do not leave your drink sitting around. Someone could put something in it like a date rape drug.

Be sure you have a way to get home that is safe. Don't accept rides with anyone who has been drinking or using drugs.

Name _____ Date _____

Free Time Safety

influence — letting others make choices for you or making them for others
temptation — the desire to do something you should avoid

Directions: Circle the answer.

1. When in public places:
    a. you can go anywhere you want
    b. talk to anyone you want
    c. stay in open places where you are safe

2. Don't talk to:
    a. anyone
    b. anyone you don't know
    c. people who look friendly

3. Don't accept a ride with:
    a. someone who has been drinking or using drugs
    b. people you trust
    c. your parents

You will have romantic relationships. They are exciting but can expose you to dangers. Relationship abuse can be physical, sexual, emotional, or verbal. There are ways to avoid these forms of abuse.

Beware of jealous and controlling behavior. When someone acts jealous and tries to control you, it is a sign of future problems.

Some people are quick to anger. When a partner gets angry a lot, that can be a sign of future abuse.

Physical Abuse:

Signs of physical abuse are bruises, sadness, depression, and fear. If you are being physically abused, tell an adult you trust.

Sexual Abuse:

Signs of sexual abuse are genital bruising, trouble sleeping, and fearfulness. If you are being abused, tell an adult you trust.

Personal

Emotional Abuse:

When a partner says mean things or yells, that is emotional abuse. Swearing and name calling are abuse too.

If you experience any of these tell someone you trust. Do not put up with abusive behavior.

Personal

Name _____ Date _____

Relationship Safety

romance — a relationship based on deep mutual affection
expose — leave you open and vulnerable
fearfulness — being afraid all the time

Directions: Circle the answer.

1. If your romantic friend acts jealous:
   a. it proves that person cares for you
   b. it can be a sign of future problems
   c. act jealous with that person too

2. Signs of physical abuse are:
   a. bruises, sadness, depression
   b. happiness and joy
   c. not having fearful behavior

3. Signs of sexual abuse are:
   a. not being fearful
   b. no problems sleeping
   c. genital brusing, trouble sleeping, fearfulness

The internet is a great way to have fun and keep in contact with friends. But it can also be dangerous if you are not careful.

To stay safe on the internet know the dangers and be careful. Always know where you're going before you go online.

Be aware of cyberbullies. Ignore mean emails or instant messages. If they continue report them to a trusted adult.

Never give name, address, phone number or email address to someone you don't know.

Never agree to meet with someone you have met on the internet.

Many people use the internet to sell services or products. Most are honest. If you are not sure ask advice from someone you trust.

Personal

Chat rooms are places to meet and talk. They are fun but can be unsafe. One danger is older adults pretending to be your age. Don't give your address, phone number, or email to strangers.

Name _____ Date _____

Internet Safety

internet — a worldwide and public computer network
cyberbullies — someone who uses the internet to bully others

Directions: Circle the answer.

1. People who use the internet to bully others are called:
    a. tech support
    b. computer geeks
    c. cyberbullies

2. Don't give your name, email or phone number to:
    a. someone you don't know on the internet
    b. even to your best friends
    c. anyone

3. If you meet someone on the internet:
    a. it's okay to meet them to get to know them better
    b. never agree to meet them somewhere
    c. that means they are okay and safe to meet somewhere

Caring for pets brings us joy and teaches responsibility. But pets can cause certain problems.

Make sure you get your pet from a reliable source. Ask a local veterinarian for reliable place to get pets.

Visit your veterinarian for regular checkups. Ask the vet how often you should come. See the vet when your pet is sick.

Be careful about other animals with whom your pet comes in contact. Some might carry diseases, even other pets.

Personal

Be gentle with your pet and get advice for its training.
Dog obedience courses are helpful in reducing aggression.

Don't allow your pet to sleep with you or to lick your cuts.
Wear gloves when cleaning the litter box.

Have your dog or cat spayed or neutered. It will keep them closer to home and reduce accidents.

Wash your hands after handling your pets.

Keep your pets away from visitors who are uncomfortable around animals. Never leave them alone with your pets.

Name _____ Date _____

Pet Safety

responsibility — being accountable for your actions
spayed — a female pet whose ovaries have been removed so she can't give birth
neutered — a male pet whose testicles have been removed so he can't impregnate a female

Directions: Circle the answer.

1. Get your pet from:
   a. a reliable source
   b. the street
   c. anywhere you want, they're all the same

2. Visit your veterinarian:
   1. only when your pet is sick
   2. any time you feel like it
   3. for regular checkups or when your pet is sick

3. Don't allow your pet to:
   a. lick your cuts
   b. have enough food
   c. drive your car when you're gone

Glossary

activate — to set in motion

appliance — household devices operated by gas or electricity

argument — a discussion with both sides disagreeing

balance — making sure the washer or dryer has an equal load on all sides

blizzard — heavy winter storm

cabinet — a storage compartment

circuit — a device that provides a path for electrical current to flow

climate — average weather in an area

combustible — easily able to catch fire

cramp — painful muscle contraction

crosswalk — a place where pedestrians cross the street

cyberbullies — someone who uses the internet to bully others

discomfort — feeling ill at ease

distract — to take your attention away from something else

drowning — when lungs fill with water causing suffocation and death

electrician — skilled tradesman who works with electrical equipment

elements — wires in electric appliances, like stoves

elements — natural things like rain that can ruin your tools

employer — someone who hires and manages workers

engine — motor that converts energy into work

equipment — a tool or device that helps you do something

exception — something that doesn't follow the usual rules

excess — too much of something

expose — leave you open and vulnerable

exposure — vulnerability to the elements

fearfulness — being afraid all the time

flammable — objects that easily catch on fire

Glossary

freedom — the ability to do what you want

hygiene — the practice of cleanliness

identification — proof of who you are

influence — letting others make choices for you or making them for others

insecticide — product to kill or keep bugs away

inspect — look at, see what condition something is in

internet — a worldwide and public computer network

issue — a point or matter of discussion

label — put on medicine bottles to tell you what is in it

laundromat — a place where you pay to wash your own clothes

leftovers — food you didn't eat but want to save

maintenance — keeping something in good working condition

medications — all kinds of medicines

neutered — a male pet whose testicles have been removed so he can't impregnate a female

obscene — bad or offensive language

outlet — wall plug-ins for electric devices

overflow — to flow or run over the top

overload — too big a load

panic — a strong and often sudden feeling of fear

pedestrian — a person who travels by foot

precautions — an action taken to prevent a problem

protective — intended to keep you safe from some danger

reflective — a surface that reflects light

reflectors — a red piece of glass worn by the bicyclist that motorists can see at night

resistant — able to tolerate certain conditions

Glossary

responsibility — being accountable for your actions

retainer — dental appliance that holds teeth in place

romance — a relationship based on deep mutual affection

rotate — to move in a circle

scrape — to rub a surface clean

sensitive — overly responsive to stimuli

separate — to keep apart

serious — dangerous, causing fear and anxiety

shallow — measuring little from top to bottom

shock — a sudden disturbance

spayed — a female pet whose ovaries have been removed so she can't give birth

stagnant — stale water that doesn't move

stretching — exercises to keep muscles loose and prevent injury

temperature — the degree of heat or cold

temptation — the desire to do something you should avoid

thorough — careful and complete

traction — to grip the surface without slipping

utensils — tools you use to eat or serve with, like forks and spoons

ventilate — to keep air moving so it's fresh

vitamin — key nutrients the body needs